ICELA

TRAVEL GUIDE

2023

An Updated Insider's Guide to Having
the Best Experience

CHRISTOPHER NELSON

CONTENTS

INTRODUCTION

Aiden had no clue what to expect when he got to Iceland. While he had heard tales of beautiful scenery, hospitable locals, and exciting experiences, nothing could have prepared him for the splendor he was about to experience.

Aiden had a thrilling sensation of freedom as he got off the aircraft and inhaled the crisp Icelandic air. The vast open areas and unending vistas seemed to spread out in front of him, beckoning him to explore.

Aiden spent the next several days riding Icelandic horses across the countryside, swimming in pristine hot springs, and hiking through magnificent volcanic landscapes. He made friends with locals and enjoyed their delectable food as they told him about the history and customs of their nation.

But there was one specific moment that won Aiden over. He was alone on a black sand beach, watching the Northern Lights dance above and the waves smash on the shore. He was filled with amazement and wonder.

Aiden realized he had discovered his happy spot at that very moment. And he was aware that he would always have a memory of Iceland's enchantment with him when he departed.

Welcome to Iceland, a country known for its breathtaking natural beauty, illustrious cultural history, and exhilarating experiences. Whether you're a seasoned traveler or a first-time visitor,

Iceland is guaranteed to wow you with its breathtaking scenery, kind people, and distinctive experiences.

You will see the strong natural forces that sculpted this enchanted land over millennia as you travel across it. Iceland's landscapes are breathtaking, with everything from towering glaciers and gushing waterfalls to bubbling hot springs and sizzling geysers.

The opportunity to see the Northern Lights, a natural light show that is as magical as it is enchanting, is one of the highlights of any vacation to Iceland. The Northern Lights are a breathtaking sight, whether you decide to view them from the luxury of a comfortable lodge or go out into the wilderness to observe them dance across the sky.

But, Iceland is much more than its natural splendors. It is a nation with a rich past and culture, where old tales are being handed down from generation to generation and where customs are firmly engrained. You will come across a kind and inviting population as you tour its quaint towns and villages. They are proud of their history and happy to share it with you.

You may sample regional specialties including Icelandic lamb, fish, and traditional skyr when visiting Iceland. You may also sample the distinctive tastes of Icelandic beer and schnapps or go to a geothermal bakery where bread is cooked in the hot earth.

Iceland has a broad variety of exhilarating activities available for anyone looking for adventure. In this untamed but stunning region, there are many activities to get your heart racing, from hiking and ice climbing to glacier excursions and snowmobiling. Also, you may go whale watching, swim in a geothermal pool, or explore the spooky beauty of a lava tunnel.

Iceland is a place unlike any other, offering a unique blend of natural splendors, cultural riches, and outdoor experiences. Now prepare to go off on a once-in-a-lifetime journey in this country of fire and ice by packing your luggage, tying your boots, and doing so.

CHAPTER ONE

ABOUT ICELAND

Geography and Climate

With geology and climate determined by its location at the meeting point of two powerful ocean currents and two tectonic plates, Iceland is a country of extremes. As a consequence, a land of breathtaking natural beauty, characterized by glaciers, volcanoes, geysers, and hot springs, was created.

Geography

Iceland is an island country in the North Atlantic Ocean that lies on the Mid-Atlantic Ridge, a divergent line where the North American and Eurasian tectonic plates collide. With over 30 active volcano systems and regular seismic activity, Iceland is one of the most volcanically active countries in the world due to its distinct geological location.

Huge lava fields, imposing glaciers, and rough mountains make up the majority of Iceland's scenery. Vatnajökull, the biggest glacier in Europe, occupies more than 8% of the nation's surface. More than 200 volcanoes may be found in Iceland, some of which have recently erupted, notably Eyjafjallajökull in 2010.

Iceland is well-known for its hot springs and geothermal sites, like the Blue Lagoon and the Geysir geysers, despite its reputation for having frigid landscapes. Iceland's position on the Mid-Atlantic Ridge, where heat from the Earth's core rises to the surface, is the cause of these natural phenomena.

Climate

Iceland's subarctic climate is characterized by cold summers and pleasant winters. Yet, because of its location in the North Atlantic, Iceland may have often occurring storms and strong wind gusts, making the weather very unpredictable and variable. Iceland's typical temperatures range from 0°C in the winter to 10°C in the summer, depending on the season.

The long summer days and short winter nights are among the most striking features of Iceland's climate. In certain locations of the nation, the sun may be seen for up to 24 hours a day during the summer, but during the winter, the reverse is true with some areas experiencing almost 24 hours of darkness.

Iceland is a well-liked holiday destination for daring tourists despite its difficult environment because of its distinctive terrain and natural beauty. Outdoor activities like hiking, ice climbing, and glacier excursions may be enjoyed against the breathtaking background of the nation's glaciers, volcanoes, and hot springs. Hence, Iceland's topography and climate provide an almost limitless number of options for discovery and adventure, whether you're hoping to see the Northern Lights, relax in a hot spring, or walk to a glacier.

History and Culture

As intriguing and distinctive as Iceland's scenery and climate are its history and culture. Iceland's culture and legacy are a combination of ancient mythology, Viking history, and modern invention, spanning from the island's founding by Norse explorers in the ninth century to the present day.

History

The earliest inhabitants of Iceland were Norse adventurers who escaped from Norway and sought safety on the island in the late ninth century. The harsh and remote surroundings of their new home had an impact on the settlers as they developed a distinctive culture and way of life. As the first parliament in history, they created the Althing, a form of government that is still in use today.

Iceland has endured many obstacles throughout the ages, such as invasions, natural catastrophes, and economic troubles. Despite these challenges, the Icelandic people have persevered and shown to be resourceful, keeping their distinctive identity and cultural history while adjusting to the times.

Culture

Icelandic culture is a synthesis of old customs and contemporary influences. It is a tiny but lively culture that has strong ties to the natural world and the striking terrain of the nation. Icelandic culture is a celebration of the creative spirit and the natural environment, from the country's music scene to its literature.

Icelandic literature has a rich history, which is one of its most remarkable features. The nation of Iceland has a long history of producing well-known writers, including Nobel laureate Halldór Laxness, and its people are voracious readers. The 13th and 14th-century Icelandic Sagas, which describe the early inhabitants of Iceland and their way of life, are some of the most well-known literary works in the whole globe.

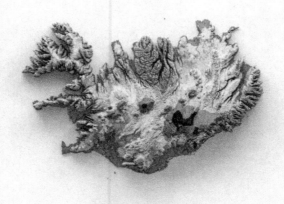

Icelandic music, which has a thriving music industry and includes a variety of genres, is another significant component of the nation's culture. Icelandic music is a reflection of the nation's originality and creative flare, ranging from the traditional sounds of Icelandic folk music to the avant-garde and experimental sounds of modern musicians.

The visual arts landscape in the nation is also growing, with several museums and galleries featuring the creations of Icelandic artists. Icelandic art is a reflection of the nation's distinctive cultural past and its present creative energy. It ranges from traditional crafts like weaving and ceramics to contemporary art installations.

Iceland's traditional foods, such as smoked lamb, pickled herring, and skyr (a sort of yogurt), reflect the nation's dependence on regional products and the necessity to preserve food for the long winter months. Iceland's location and climate also have an impact on its cuisine.

In conclusion, Iceland's landscape, climate, and history are all distinctive and intriguing. Iceland's culture is an ode to imagination, fortitude, and the natural environment. This is evident in everything from its Viking past to its literary legacy, its thriving music industry to its cutting-edge art sector. Icelanders are hospitable and pleasant people who are ready to share their history with the rest of the world.

Getting Around

Traveling about Iceland is a crucial component of any trip there, whether you're seeing the breathtaking natural landscapes or learning about the diverse culture and history of the place. It is simple to travel across Iceland and take advantage of everything that the nation has to offer thanks to the number of transportation choices that are accessible, including public transit and vehicle rentals.

Hire cars

One of the most common methods of transportation in Iceland is automobile rental, which enables independent exploration of the nation's numerous gorgeous roads and undiscovered attractions. The airport and major towns like Reykjavik are home to a significant number of automobile rental agencies that provide a wide range of vehicles, from little-budget cars to bigger SUVs and four-wheel-drive vehicles. It's crucial to keep in mind, too, that driving in Iceland may be difficult, particularly in the winter when the roads can be slippery and dangerous. Thus, for increased security and dependability, renting a four-wheel-drive vehicle is strongly advised.

Using Public Transit

Moreover, Iceland boasts a dependable public transportation network that connects the majority of significant towns and cities via buses and coaches. A robust bus system links the city's many sites and attractions, including the well-known Blue Lagoon, in Reykjavik in particular. Also, there are regular bus excursions that take tourists on day trips to well-known tourist hotspots including the South Coast and the Golden Circle.

Taxis:
In all of Iceland's main cities and towns, taxis are readily accessible. Licensed taxis are easily recognized by the yellow roof sign. But, they may be pricey, particularly for longer trips, so it's worth asking the driver for an estimate or double-checking the rate before you leave.

Internal Flights:
Moreover, Iceland boasts a sophisticated domestic airline network that connects the main towns and cities regularly. If you're short on time or wish to go to some of Iceland's more isolated regions that are not readily accessible by car, flying is a terrific choice. Flights may be costly, particularly during the busiest travel season, so it's vital to reserve well in advance to get the best deals.

Tours
Last but not least, guided tours are a fantastic way to see Iceland, particularly if you don't have much time or want to see the most well-known sights with the

assistance of a knowledgeable tour guide. Many tour companies provide a range of excursions, including day trips and multi-day journeys that takes in some of Iceland's most breathtaking vistas and natural marvels, such as the Northern Lights, glaciers, and waterfalls.

Traveling to Iceland is rather simple, and there are several transportation alternatives to meet all travel tastes and price ranges. Whether you decide to fly domestically, take a public bus or cab, hire a vehicle, and explore independently, or sign up for a guided tour, you will undoubtedly have an incredible time in this magnificent nation.

CHAPTER TWO

Planning Your Trip

When to Visit Iceland

The time of your visit is quite important when organizing a vacation to Iceland. All through the year, Iceland sees a vast diversity of weather, with each season providing a distinctive selection of experiences and activities for tourists. Based on the seasons and weather in Iceland, here is detailed advice on the best time to go there.

Summer (June through August)

In Iceland, the summer is the busiest travel period, and with good reason. It's the ideal time of year to visit the nation's numerous natural treasures, including the well-known Golden Circle, glaciers, and waterfalls, thanks to the long days and pleasant weather. The normal temperature is between 10°C and 15°C (50°F and 59°F), and there are very long days with up to 24 hours of sunshine in certain places. As a result, now is the ideal time to go hiking, camping, whale watching, and doing road trips.

Fall (September through November)

If you want to visit Iceland without dealing with the summertime crowds, autumn is a fantastic time to go. The temperature drops to between 5°C and 10°C (41°F and 50°F), and the daylight hours start to become shorter. Yet late September marks the start of the Northern Lights season, allowing visitors to see the aurora borealis, one of nature's most beautiful displays.

Winter (December to February)

Short days, long nights, and frigid temperatures define Icelandic winter. It's also the finest time to see the Northern Lights, which are quite beautiful. The country's typical temperature is between -1°C and 4°C (30°F and 39°F), and although the weather might make it difficult to move, the winter scenery is quite stunning. Wintertime is a great time for sports including skiing, snowmobiling, and ice carving.

Spring (March to May)

Icelandic spring is known for its frequently shifting weather patterns and temperatures that range from 0°C to 8°C (32°F to 46°F). The winter snow starts to melt as the days become longer, exposing a landscape covered with wildflowers and lush foliage. If you want to view newborn animals, like lambs, spring is a terrific time to go. It's also a great time to see the Northern Lights before the season finishes in mid-April.

 Iceland is a place that is accessible throughout the year, with each season providing a distinctive range of experiences and activities. While the summer months, when the weather is nice and the days are long, are the busiest for tourists, there are still plenty of chances to take in Iceland's natural beauty in the cooler months of autumn, winter, and spring. The ideal time to visit Iceland ultimately depends on your interests and tastes, so it's important to check the weather and popular seasonal activities before making travel arrangements.

Visa Requirements

Some nationalities may need a visa to enter Iceland. To prevent any problems at the border, it is important to confirm the Iceland visa requirements before making travel arrangements. Below is a detailed explanation of Iceland's travel visa requirements.

Schengen Area

Iceland belongs to the Schengen Area, a group of 26 European nations that have done away with passport checks and other forms of border control at its shared borders. Visitors from Schengen Area nations may visit Iceland without a visa and remain there for up to 90 days during 180 days.

Non-Schengen Area

Iceland may need a visa for visitors from non-Schengen countries. Citizens of nations including the United States, Canada, Australia, and Japan are included in this. Depending on the visitor's nationality, the intended length and purpose of the trip, and the visa criteria, there are several visa application procedures.

Brief Stay Visa

If you're a citizen of a non-Schengen nation and you want to go to Iceland for up to 90 days during 180 days, you may need to apply for a short-stay visa. Visitors may enter Iceland with this visa for leisure, business, or family travel.

Long-Stay Permit

You must apply for a long-stay visa if you want to remain in Iceland for more than 90 days. This kind of visa enables travelers to remain in Iceland for employment, education, or family reunion.

Application Methods

You must apply for a visa in advance at the Icelandic embassy or consulate in your nation of residence. Applicants normally need to provide a current passport, a completed visa application form, and evidence of sufficient funds to pay the cost of the trip. A trip schedule, travel insurance, and evidence of lodging may also be needed.

Visa-Waiver program

The Visa Waiver Program, which allows tourists to remain in Iceland for up to 90 days without a visa, may be available to citizens of a few nations, including the United States, Canada, and Australia. Visitors must possess a machine-readable passport, a return or onward ticket, and travel insurance to be admitted.

To prevent any issues at the border, it is crucial to confirm visa requirements before making travel plans to Iceland. Visitors from Schengen Area nations may visit Iceland without a visa and remain there for up to 90 days during 180 days. Depending on how long they want to stay and what they intend to do while there, visitors from outside the Schengen Area may need a short- or long-stay visa. A current passport, a completed visa application form, and evidence of sufficient funds to pay the cost of the trip are normally required for the application procedure. Citizens of a few nations may apply for the Visa Waiver Program, which enables visitors to Iceland to stay up to 90 days without a visa.

Currency and Money Matters

The Icelandic krona (ISK), which is divisible into 100 aurar, is the country of Iceland's official currency. Travelers to Iceland should be knowledgeable about currency conversion rates and smart methods to manage their money while traveling.

Converting Money

Throughout Iceland, banks, post offices, and currency exchange offices are available for foreign currency conversion. Also widespread are ATMs, many of which take credit and debit cards from other countries. When converting money, it is crucial to examine the exchange rates and fees since certain locations could charge more than others.

Charge cards

Iceland accepts credit cards extensively, so tourists may use them to make purchases and get cash from ATMs. The most widely used credit cards are Visa and MasterCard, however, American Express and other credit cards may not be accepted everywhere. Before leaving, it's crucial to inquire about international transaction fees with your credit card company and let them know about your vacation plans to prevent any problems with card use.

Cash

Even though credit cards are often accepted in Iceland, it's still a good idea to carry extra cash with you for petty purchases or unexpected situations. Visitors may exchange currencies at banks or exchange offices or withdraw cash using ATMs and debit cards.

Tipping

In Iceland, tips are seldom given since most items and services come with a service fee already. To show thanks, it's appropriate to round up the entire cost of a meal or service.

VAT: Value-Added Tax

The value-added tax (VAT) rate in Iceland is 24%, and it is reflected in the cost of the majority of products and services. By submitting their receipts and completing the required documentation at the airport before departure, visitors who are not citizens of the European Union (EU) may request a refund on the VAT they paid for goods made in Iceland.

Travelers visiting Iceland should be aware of the Icelandic krona, which serves as the nation's official currency, as well as the best methods to manage money while traveling. Credit cards are readily accepted, and there are several banks, ATMs, and currency exchange offices. While it is uncommon in

Iceland to tip, it is nonetheless appropriate to round up the bill as a sign of gratitude. Presenting their receipts and completing the required documentation at the airport before leaving, non-EU citizens may get a VAT refund for goods made in Iceland.

Travel Insurance

Everyone contemplating a vacation to Iceland should take travel insurance into account. While travel insurance is not required when visiting Iceland, it is strongly advised to protect yourself against unforeseen costs and situations that may occur during your vacation. We'll discuss the advantages of travel insurance and what to consider while choosing coverage in this article.

Travel insurance benefits include:
Medical crises, trip cancellation or interruption, lost or stolen baggage, and other unforeseen expenditures are all commonly covered by travel insurance. Certain insurance plans could also cover popular Icelandic sports like skiing, snowmobiling, and glacier trekking.

Medical Emergencies
Travel insurance may cover medical costs, such as hospitalization, doctor visits, and prescription medication if you become sick or hurt while visiting

Iceland. If you need medical care that is unavailable in Iceland or need to be transferred home for treatment, this coverage may also include emergency medical evacuation.

Trip Cancellation
Travel insurance may cover the cost of your vacation, including airfare, lodging, and activities if you have to postpone or cancel your trip due to unexpected events like sickness, accident, or a family emergency.

Loss or Theft of Baggage
If your goods are lost or stolen while you're traveling, travel insurance may also cover lost or stolen bags. This coverage may cover the cost of replacing your goods as well as the costs of buying essentials like clothes and toiletries.

Selecting a Policy
It's crucial to take your unique requirements and the activities you have planned for your vacation into account when choosing travel insurance coverage for your trip to Iceland. For instance, it's crucial to get insurance that covers outdoor pursuits like a snowmobile or glacier trekking if you want to partake in these activities. To make sure you have enough protection, you should also think about the

policy's coverage limitations, deductibles, and exclusions.

Also, it's crucial to keep in mind that certain credit cards come with travel insurance as a perk. As a result, before getting separate coverage, be sure to check with your credit card company.

Everyone contemplating a vacation to Iceland must take travel insurance into account. It offers protection against unforeseen costs and crises, such as medical problems, trip interruptions or cancellations, lost or stolen baggage, and travel-related issues. While choosing insurance, it's crucial to take into account your unique requirements and the activities you have planned for your vacation. You should also carefully study the coverage limits, deductibles, and exclusions of the policy to make sure you have enough protection.

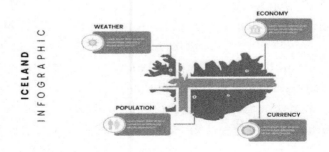

CHAPTER THREE

TOP ATTRACTIONS IN ICELAND

Reykjavik

Iceland's capital and biggest city, Reykjavik, is a dynamic, contemporary metropolis with a rich cultural heritage. It is the center of the social, cultural, and economic life of the nation and has a population of slightly over 130,000. Reykjavik is the ideal place from which to explore the rest of the nation since it provides a distinctive blend of urban sophistication and natural beauty.

Some of the great places to go in Reykjavik are listed below:

Hallgrimskirkja: This beautiful church is a must-see site and one of Reykjavik's most recognizable structures. It took over 50 years to construct and was named after the priest and poet Hallgrimur Petursson, who was from Iceland and lived in the 17th century. The church's striking architecture, which includes a colossal white concrete façade and a distinctive pipe organ, was inspired by the volcanic rocks that can be found naturally across Iceland.

Harpa Concert Hall: Iceland's top music hall and conference facility are housed in the spectacular glass structure known as Harpa Concert Hall, which is situated on Reykjavik's waterfront. For both music fans and culture vultures, it is a must-visit location because of its distinctive architectural style and top-notch acoustics.

The Sun Voyager: The Sun Voyager is a famous sculpture that honors Iceland's Viking past and is situated on the city's waterfront. The Sun Voyager, a magnificent depiction of a Viking ship created by artist Jon Gunnar Arnason, represents the nation's past as well as the bravery and spirit of its people.

The National Museum of Iceland: This museum, which is situated in the heart of Reykjavik, provides a thorough examination of Iceland's history and culture from the time of the Vikings to the present. It is an interesting and instructive location with exhibitions ranging from prehistoric relics and medieval manuscripts to modern art and photography.

The Perlan Museum: Dedicated to Iceland's natural beauties and the forces that define its environment, this futuristic museum is situated on a hill overlooking Reykjavik. For anybody interested in Iceland's geology, geography, and ecology, this attraction is a must-visit since it has interactive exhibits, multimedia displays, and a 360-degree observation deck.

The Reykjavik Art Museum: The Reykjavik Art Museum is a showcase of Iceland's thriving contemporary art scene. It has three venues across the city. It is a must-see for art lovers and culture vultures, with a collection that ranges from sculpture and painting to video and installation art.

Laugardalslaug: Laugardalslaug is a huge outdoor swimming facility on the outskirts of Reykjavik that is well-liked by both residents and tourists. It is the ideal location to unwind and rest after a day of touring since it has heated pools, hot tubs, saunas, and steam rooms.

The Reykjavik City Walk: The Reykjavik City Walk is an excellent opportunity to learn about the history, culture, and architecture of Reykjavik. It is a free walking tour led by locals. A great introduction to the city for first-time visitors, the trip includes some of the city's most recognizable sights, such as the Parliament building, city hall, and the old port.

A bustling and friendly city, Reykjavik provides a special blend of culture, history, and scenic beauty. Reykjavik is the ideal place to begin your Icelandic experience, whether your interests include visiting the city's museums and galleries, relaxing in its hot springs, or taking a day excursion to see the local countryside.

The Golden Circle

Almost 300 kilometers of the road make up the famed Golden Circle tourist route in Iceland, which features some of the nation's most beautiful natural marvels and stunning landscapes. The Thingvellir National Park, the Geysir geothermal region, and the Gullfoss waterfall are three of Iceland's most well-known tourist destinations, making up the "Golden Circle" circuit.

The Golden Circle may be easily visited in one day from Reykjavik by self-driving, bus excursions, or guided tours. There are a ton of other attractions along the way, such as old churches, hot springs, and charming villages.

The major attractions in The Golden Circle are broken down in the following manner:

Thingvellir National Park: Thingvellir is an important historical site for Icelanders and a UNESCO World Heritage Site. The Althing, the first parliament in history, was founded there in the year 930. Thingvellir is now a magnificent natural park with a vast lake Thingvallavatn, deep fissures, and lovely waterfalls. The Mid-Atlantic Ridge, where the North American and Eurasian tectonic plates converge, may also be seen in the park.

The park's pathways allow for strolls, historical site exploration, and even the opportunity to swim or scuba dive in the pristine waters of the tectonic plate rift known as Silfra.

Geysir Geothermal Area: The Strokkur geyser, known for its frequent eruptions of boiling water up to 30 meters in the air, is located in the Geysir geothermal region. Several geysers, including the original Geysir, which has been inactive since 1916, may be found nearby.

Moreover, there are bubbling hot springs, steam vents, and vibrant mineral deposits in the vicinity. In addition to taking a dip in the surrounding hot springs, visitors may stroll along the boardwalks to witness the geothermal activity.

Gullfoss Waterfall: One of Iceland's most recognizable natural beauties is the Gullfoss waterfall, sometimes referred to as the "Golden Waterfall." The Hvita River, which flows down two tiers and plunges a total of 32 meters into a tight canyon, creates the waterfall.

There are numerous observation platforms where visitors may watch the waterfall, and each one provides a different angle of the falls. Visitors may watch the whole cascade from the top of the falls, which is the most popular vantage point.

Additional Attractions

In addition to the three primary landmarks, The Golden Circle also includes several additional noteworthy locations, such as:

- Keri Crater Lake: Surrounded by red volcanic rock, this lake's vivid blue water is a breathtaking sight.
- Skálholt Church: This ancient building was formerly Iceland's main place of worship and had a significant impact on its history.

- The geothermal baths at Laugarvatn, notably Fontana Spa, which has outdoor hot tubs and saunas, are well-known.
- Hverageri: With several hot springs and geothermal parks, this town is dubbed the "Hot Spring Capital of Iceland."

All in all, The Golden Circle is a wonderful chance to see some of Iceland's most stunning natural beauties and ancient sites. The Golden Circle in Iceland is a must-see location, regardless of your interests in geology, history, or just admiring the breathtaking nature.

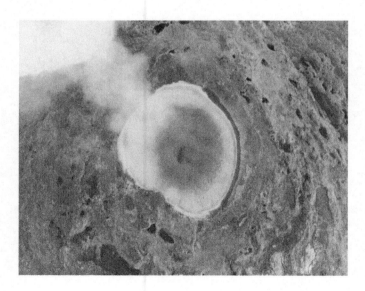

The Blue Lagoon

One of Iceland's most well-known tourist destinations, the Blue Lagoon draws tourists from all over the globe. This geothermal spa, which is approximately 40 minutes' drive from Reykjavik and is situated in a lava field on the Reykjanes Peninsula, is well-known for its milky blue waters that are nutrient- and mineral-rich.

The Blue Lagoon is covered in the following comprehensive guide:

History

The Blue Lagoon was unintentionally created in 1976 when an adjacent lava field started to fill with extra water from a local geothermal power station. Warm water combined with the silica-rich soil creates the lagoon's distinctive blue tint, which has earned it worldwide fame.

Minerals including silica, algae, and sulfur are abundant in the lagoon's water and are said to have healing effects on the skin. Many tourists visit the lagoon in search of relaxation and renewal, and many are convinced of its therapeutic benefits.

Facilities

A range of amenities is available in the Blue Lagoon to improve the guest experience, such as:

The lagoon itself, which has a size of roughly 8,000 square meters and is nourished by the adjacent geothermal plant, is the major draw. The water is full of minerals that are said to be excellent for the skin and are maintained at a moderate temperature of 38–40°C throughout the year.

Spa: The Blue Lagoon Spa provides a variety of services, such as body cleanses, facials, and massages. The treatments feed and renew the skin by using the lagoon's mineral-rich water as well as additional all-natural components like algae and silica.

Restaurants: The Blue Lagoon is home to several eateries, including LAVA Restaurant, which provides gourmet dining with lagoon views. A café and a bar are also present, both of which sell drinks created with the mineral-rich water of the lagoon.

Shop: The Blue Lagoon features a store where guests may buy skincare items manufactured with the minerals of the lagoon and other organic components.

The Blue Lagoon excursion

The Blue Lagoon is accessible all year round and provides various activities depending on the season.

Visitors may take advantage of the prolonged daylight hours and the chance to explore the neighborhood throughout the summer (June to August). It's advisable to make reservations in advance during this season since the lagoon is often busier.

Visitors may take in the northern lights and the joyous holiday mood from November through February. This makes it a more tranquil and pleasant experience, and the lagoon is also less congested.

Guests have a variety of ticket choices to select from, including:
Basic Admission: Includes a towel and access to the lagoon.

Access to the lagoon, a towel, and a bathrobe are all included with premium admission, along with a drink and a table at the LAVA Restaurant.

Retreat Spa: Provides a personal host, access to a private lagoon, and several spa services.

Visitor Advice for the Blue Lagoon

The Blue Lagoon is a well-liked attraction, so it's important to reserve in advance to guarantee availability.

- Carry a swimsuit: Swimsuits must be worn at all times while in the lagoon and are available for purchase or rental at the establishment.

- Keep your valuables at home: It is advised to leave jewelry at home or in a locker since the minerals in the lagoon might harm it.

- The facility's restrictions, which forbid diving or leaping into the water as well as bringing glass or other sharp items into the lagoon, must be followed. Guests are requested to take a shower before entering the lagoon.

Ultimately, visiting The Blue Lagoon is a life-changing experience that provides rest, renewal, and a singular window into Iceland's geothermal ecosystem. Warm, mineral-rich water combined with breathtaking scenery results in a genuinely spectacular experience that shouldn't be missed.

Vatnajökull Glacier National Park

The biggest glacier in Europe may be found at Vatnajökull Glacier National Park, one of Iceland's most magnificent natural marvels. The park, which is located in the southeast of Iceland, is well-known for its rocky landscapes, ice landscapes, and breathtaking glaciers. It has a total size of roughly 14,000 square kilometers.

A comprehensive guide to Vatnajökull Glacier National Park is provided below:

History

Established in 2008, the Vatnajökull Glacier National Park spans a sizable area of southeast Iceland. The park, which is home to several rare and threatened plant and animal species, was established to preserve the region's distinctive natural environment and cultural history.

The biggest glacier in Europe, Vatnajökull Glacier, which makes up around 8% of Iceland's landmass, is the inspiration for the park's name. The glacier plays a significant role in the environment of Iceland and is a significant supply of fresh water for the area.

Attractions

Visitors to Vatnajökull Glacier National Park may engage in a variety of attractions and activities, such as:

- Glacier hiking is one of the most well-liked activities in the park. Tourists may explore the glaciers, frozen landscapes, and breathtaking ice caves on guided trips.

- Ice Climbing: For climbers with greater expertise, ice climbing is also an option. With the aid of a guide, visitors may scale the park's high ice cliffs and frozen waterfalls.

- The park is among the greatest sites in Iceland to see the Northern Lights. Take a trip to view the Aurora Borealis and take in the sky's natural light display.

⊥ Jökulsárlón Glacial Lagoon is a breathtaking natural marvel and a must-see for tourists. It is situated on the southern fringe of the park. Icebergs that have detached from the glacier and are floating in the lagoon's pure water are in plenty.

⊥ Skaftafell Nature Reserve: Situated in the southern section of the park, the Skaftafell Nature Reserve is renowned for its gorgeous hiking paths, waterfalls, and breathtaking scenery.

Vatnajökull Glacier National Park Escursion

The ideal time to visit Vatnajökull Glacier National Park depends on the activities you're interested in. The park is open all year. Visitors may take advantage of winter activities like skiing and snowmobiling as well as the Northern Lights throughout the winter months (November to February). Visitors may engage in outdoor activities like hiking, camping, and other ones throughout the summer (June to August).

Visitors may drive or take a bus from Reykjavik, which is roughly a 5-hour journey away, to get to the park. Moreover, guided trips with activities and transportation are offered.

Visitor Advice for the National Park of Vatnajökull Glacier

⤓ Warm clothing is recommended since the park is often chilly. Bring a waterproof jacket as well.

⤓ Employ a guide: It's advisable to hire a guide who can show you the finest paths and keep you safe for activities like glacier trekking and ice climbing.

⤓ Respect the environment: Since the park is a protected area, visitors are encouraged to show respect for it by avoiding upsetting the animals or vegetation.

⤓ Be ready: Due to the park's isolation, it's crucial to pack lots of food and drink, as well as any equipment required for camping or trekking.

Overall, both nature lovers and adventure seekers should visit Iceland's Vatnajökull Glacier National Park. It's an experience that will stick with you for the rest of your life because of the breathtaking glaciers, freezing landscapes, and extraordinary natural treasures.

Skaftafell Nature Reserve

One of Iceland's most well-known natural features is Skaftafell Natural Reserve, which is situated in the country's southeast. The 1,500-square-kilometer reserve is well-known for its breathtaking scenery, hiking routes, and exceptional natural features.

This is a comprehensive guide with all the information you want about Skaftafell Natural Reserve:

History

In 2008, the 1967-founded Skaftafell Natural Reserve was merged with the Vatnajökull Glacier National Park. The reserve, which is home to several rare and threatened plant and animal species, was established to safeguard the region's distinctive natural environment and cultural history.

Attractions

Visitors may engage in a variety of attractions and activities in Skaftafell Natural Reserve, such as:

+ Paths for Hiking: The reserve is renowned for its stunning hiking routes, which vary from short strolls to longer hikes. The Skaftafellsjökull Glacier Trail, the Svartifoss Waterfall Trail, and the Kristnartindar Mountain Trail are a few of the most well-known paths.

+ Waterfalls: Many magnificent waterfalls can be found inside the reserve, notably Svartifoss, which is renowned for its distinctive basalt columns.

+ The Vatnajökull Glacier, the biggest glacier in Europe, is one of several glaciers that are close to the reserve.

+ Wildlife: Many animal species, including reindeer, Arctic foxes, and other bird species, call the reserve home.

Skaftafell Natural Reserve Excursion

The ideal time to visit Skaftafell Natural Reserve depends on the activities you're interested in. The reserve is open all year. Visitors may engage in outdoor activities like hiking and other ones throughout the summer (June to August). Visitors may engage in winter activities like skiing and snowmobiling from November through February.

Visitors may drive or take a bus from Reykjavik, which is roughly a 5-hour journey away, to reach the reserve. Moreover, guided trips with activities and transportation are offered.

A Few Travel Suggestions for Skaftafell Natural Reserve

- Be prepared to layer your clothing and carry a waterproof jacket since Icelandic weather may be erratic.

- Employ a guide: It's advisable to hire a guide for activities like glacier trekking so they can show you the safest ways and keep you informed.

- The reserve is a protected area, thus visitors are requested to respect nature by not disturbing the animals or plants there.

- Get ready: Due to the reserve's isolation, it's crucial to pack lots of food, water, and other equipment needed for camping or trekking.

Overall, for nature lovers and outdoor enthusiasts, Iceland's Skaftafell Natural Reserve is a must-visit location. It's an experience that will stick with you for a lifetime because of its breathtaking scenery, hiking routes, and distinctive natural beauty.

Jökulsárlón Glacier Lagoon

In the southeast of Iceland, there lies a breathtaking natural marvel called Jökulsárlón Glacial Lagoon. Due to its distinctive beauty and beautiful surroundings, it is one of the most visited tourist destinations in the nation.

An extensive guide to Jökulsárlón Glacier Lagoon information is provided below:

History

In the 1930s, glaciers began to melt, creating Jökulsárlón Glacier Lagoon. A sizable lake with icebergs and crystal pure water was created after the glaciers melted. The lagoon now supports a diverse range of marine life, including seals and several fish species.

Attractions

Visitors may engage in a variety of attractions and activities in Jökulsárlón Glacial Lagoon, such as:

- Boat Tours: To get a closer look at the icebergs and animals, visitors may take boat trips around the lagoon. Experienced tour guides who are knowledgeable about the history and ecology of the region lead the excursions.

- Glacier Walks: Tourists may embark on guided glacier treks to investigate the lagoon's surroundings. These hikes provide guests with a unique viewpoint of the breathtaking surroundings and give them a chance to come close to the icebergs.

- Wildlife Observation: A diversity of marine life, including seals, fish, and several bird species, may be seen in the lagoon. These creatures may be seen by visitors from the beach or while on a boat excursion.

The lagoon is a well-liked location for photographers since it provides breathtaking views and unusual lighting. Tourists may take beautiful pictures of the icebergs and the surrounding area.

Jökulsárlón Glacier Lagoon Excursion

The ideal time to visit Jökulsárlón Glacial Lagoon depends on the activities you're interested in. The lagoon is available all year. Visitors may take advantage of boat trips and other outdoor activities throughout the summer (June to August). Visitors may take in the breathtaking surroundings and distinctive lights throughout the winter months (November to February).

Visitors may go to the lagoon by car or bus from Reykjavik, which is approximately a five-hour trip away. Moreover, guided trips with activities and transportation are offered.

Jökulsárlón Glacier Lagoon Travel Advice

- Be careful to pack a waterproof jacket and dress warmly since Iceland's weather may be brisk and changeable.

- Hire a guide: It's advisable to hire a guide for activities like glacier treks who can show you the finest ways and keep you safe.

- The lagoon is a protected area, thus visitors are requested to respect nature by not disturbing the animals or plants there.

🔸 Get ready: Due to the lagoon's isolation, it's crucial to pack lots of food, water, and other equipment needed for camping or trekking.

Overall, for nature lovers and outdoor enthusiasts, Iceland's Jökulsárlón Glacial Lagoon is a must-visit location. It's an experience you won't forget because of its breathtaking beauty and distinctive attractions.

The Northern Lights

One of the most amazing natural occurrences on earth is the Northern Lights, sometimes referred to as the Aurora Borealis. It's not surprising that Iceland is one of the top tourist destinations in the world since it's one of the greatest spots to view the Northern Lights. This comprehensive resource will tell you all you need to know about Iceland's Northern Lights.

The Northern Lights: What are they?

In the northern areas, there is a natural light show known as the Northern Lights. They result from solar particles that are electrically charged slamming with airborne particles on Earth. As these particles collide, the sky is illuminated with a stunning and vibrant show of lights.

When can I go to Iceland to view the Northern Lights?

In Iceland, September through April is the greatest period to observe the Northern Lights, with December to February being the finest. The evenings are longer during these months, increasing your possibility of viewing the Northern Lights. While there is no certainty of seeing the Northern Lights since they are natural phenomena, your chances are better during these months.

Where in Iceland can I view the Northern Lights?

Iceland is a country where the Northern Lights may be viewed, although it is better to go where there is less light pollution and a clear sky.

The following are some of Iceland's top locations to see the Northern Lights:

+ Thingvellir National Park is a UNESCO World Heritage Site and a well-known location to see the Northern Lights.

+ Reykjanes Peninsula is an isolated region with no light pollution, making it an excellent location to see the Northern Lights.

- Because of its clean sky and little light pollution, Akureyri, a city in northern Iceland, is a well-known location for witnessing the Northern Lights.

- In addition to being a major tourist destination in Iceland, the Jökulsárlón Glacial Lagoon is a fantastic place to see the Northern Lights.

In Iceland, how do you view the Northern Lights?

In Iceland, there are a few different methods to observe the Northern Lights:

- Take a guided trip: Several tour companies provide Northern Lights excursions in Iceland. The greatest viewing locations are often included in these trips, which also provide educated experts who can explain the phenomenon's underlying science.

- Renting a vehicle is a terrific alternative if you want to go exploring on your own. This gives you the freedom to seek the Northern Lights whenever and wherever you choose without being constrained by a guided tour.

- Consider living in a distant area that is free of light pollution if you want to increase your probability of viewing the Northern Lights. Iceland is home to several outlying lodges and cottages that provide breathtaking views of the Northern Lights.

Icelandic Northern Lights viewing advice

- Look at the weather: The Northern Lights are best seen on clear evenings, so look at the forecast before making travel arrangements.

- Be sure to pack a waterproof jacket and dress warmly since it is better to see the Northern Lights in the middle of the night.

- Be patient: As the Northern Lights are natural phenomena, they cannot be predicted in advance.

- Put your phone in airplane mode or turn it off if you want to see the Northern Lights. Your phone generates light that may interfere with your ability to see them.

In conclusion, seeing the Northern Lights in Iceland is an experience of a lifetime that you won't want to miss. One of the world's most amazing natural displays is possible to see with the correct preparation and a little bit of luck.

Whale Watching

One of Iceland's most popular tourist attractions is whale watching. This spectacular species may be found in abundance in the nation because of its special position between the North Atlantic and Arctic Oceans.

Where in Iceland can you watch whales?

Icelandic seas are home to more than 20 distinct kinds of whales. Among the most typical ones are:

1. The most often-seen whales in Iceland are humpback whales. They are well-known for their acrobatic performances and their recognizable flukes, which are often visible as they dive.

2. The second most frequent whale in Iceland is the minke whale. They are recognized for

their speed and agility and are smaller than humpback whales.

3. The biggest mammal in the world, blue whales are sometimes sighted in Icelandic seas, but they are not as frequent as humpbacks and minkes.

4. Orcas: Also referred to as killer whales, these animals are dolphins. They are renowned for their cunning and hunting prowess.

What time of year is ideal for whale viewing in Iceland?

May through September is the ideal season to go whale watching in Iceland. It is easier to detect whales during these months due to warmer weather and often calmer water conditions. While whale sightings are never certain, it's vital to remember that your chances are better during these months.

Where in Iceland can you go whale watching?

You can go whale watching in a few different places in Iceland. Among the most well-liked ones are:

Iceland's most well-liked starting location for whale-watching cruises is Reykjavik. Typically, tours leave from the ancient harbor and transport you to Faxaflói Bay.

Hsavk: This little settlement in northern Iceland is renowned as the country's center for whale viewing. Tours that take you to Skjálfandi Bay leave from the port.

Another well-liked location for whale viewing is in the northern Icelandic city of Akureyri. Typically, tours take you to the Eyjafjörur fjord from the port.

How can I see whales in Iceland?

In Iceland, there are various options for whale watching:

- Join a guided trip: Several tour companies provide whale-watching excursions in Iceland. These excursions typically run between two and three hours and include educated guides who can identify the various whale species and provide fascinating information about them.

- Private charter: You may hire a private boat for your whale-watching excursion if you'd like a more secluded experience.

- If you don't want to take a boat, you may see whales from the ground. The cliffs at Látrabjarg in the Westfjords and the village of Hólmavk in the northwest are some of the greatest locations to accomplish this.

Advice for seeing whales in Iceland

- Dress warmly: The weather on the lake may be cool even in the summer, so be sure you wear warm layers and carry a waterproof jacket.

- The guide will be able to advise you where to look and what to be on the lookout for, so pay close attention to their directions.

- Be patient: It's possible that you won't see any whales when whale watching, so be ready to wait.

- Remember to handle the whales with respect; they are wild creatures and should be treated as such. Don't go too close and don't bother them.

Overall, whale watching in Iceland is an exhilarating and unique experience. It's an opportunity to see the magnificence of these animals, whether you see a humpback breaching or a minke swimming beside the boat.

CHAPTER FOUR

Outdoor Activities in Iceland

Hiking and Trekking

In Iceland, hiking and trekking are among the most well-liked outdoor pursuits, and with good reason. The landscapes of Iceland are among the most beautiful and varied in the world, and walking through them is an experience unlike any other. An extensive guide to everything you need to know about hiking and trekking in Iceland is provided below:

In Iceland, when is the ideal season to go hiking and trekking?

The summer season, which lasts from June through August, is the ideal time to go hiking and trekking in Iceland. The longer days and warmer weather throughout this season provide extra daylight for exploring. It's crucial to keep in mind that Icelandic weather may be unexpected, especially in the summer, so you should always be ready for anything.

Where in Iceland can you go climbing and trekking?

In Iceland, there are various hiking and trekking routes, from short day walks to extended expeditions. Among the most well-liked ones are:

Landmannalaugar: The magnificent, multicolored mountains and hot springs in this region of the Icelandic Highlands are well-known. There are several hiking paths around that range in difficulty.

One of Iceland's most well-known hiking routes is the **Laugavegur Trail,** and with good reason. The 55-kilometer track passes through some of Iceland's most breathtaking scenery, including vibrant mountains, glaciers, and hot springs.

Skaftafell National Park is a hiker's paradise with a variety of easy-to-difficulty paths. It is located in southern Iceland. Glaciers, waterfalls, and breathtaking mountain vistas make the park famous.

The Westfjords' Hornstrandir Nature Reserve, which can only be reached by boat, is a sanctuary for hikers seeking an experience that is genuinely off the beaten road. Arctic animals may be found there as well as a rocky beach and high cliffs.

Where can I hike and trek in Iceland?

In Iceland, there are various methods to go hiking and trekking:

- Join a guided trip: Several tour companies are offering guided hiking and trekking excursions in Iceland. These trips include skilled tour guides who can point out the greatest locations and share relevant local information.

- Rent a vehicle and go exploring independently: Iceland is famed for its breathtaking landscapes, and one of the best ways to see them is by traveling the nation in a car. You may explore various hiking paths and beautiful locations on your own.

- The majority of Iceland's hiking paths feature mountain cabins where you may spend the night. These huts provide a unique and immersive way to see the Icelandic environment and are furnished with basic conveniences like beds and kitchens.

Iceland hiking & trekking advice

+ Be ready for anything: Iceland's weather, even at the height of summer, is erratic, so pack plenty of warm, waterproof gear as well as strong hiking boots.

+ Respect the environment: The delicate ecosystem of Iceland should be handled carefully and respectfully. Follow the designated pathways and don't damage the animals or the plants.

+ Iceland's wildness should be preserved since it is pure and should not be disturbed. Pack out all of your rubbish carefully and leave no trace.

+ Know your limits: Hiking and trekking in Iceland may be difficult, so be careful to be mindful of your limitations and take rests as necessary.

Overall, Iceland's hiking and trekking are fantastic adventures that let you completely immerse yourself in the nation's breathtaking scenery. Iceland's natural beauty is certain to make an impact, whether you're trekking through the lonely solitude of Hornstrandir or exploring the vibrant highlands of Landmannalaugar.

Glacier Hiking and Ice Climbing

The most exhilarating outdoor sports in Iceland include ice climbing and glacier trekking. Iceland has some of the most breathtaking glacial landscapes in the world, with over 4,000 glaciers covering 11% of the nation. Here is a thorough reference on all you need to know about ice climbing and glacier trekking in Iceland:

What is trekking on glaciers?

Walking on glaciers, which are enormous accumulations of ice and snow that move slowly over time, is known as glacier trekking. Hiking on glaciers offers a unique and breathtaking view of the scenery as well as the chance to personally see the impacts of climate change.

Where in Iceland can you go glacier hiking?

In Iceland, you may undertake glacier hiking on several glaciers, including:

The Vatnajökull Glacier, which occupies more than 8% of Iceland's area, is the country's biggest glacier. On a glacier trek, you may see some of the area's breathtaking ice formations and ice caves.

The second-largest glacier in Iceland, **Langjökull Glacier,** is renowned for its breathtaking blue ice sculptures. A guided trip may be taken to a man-made ice tunnel that is located there.

The Sólheimajökull Glacier, one of the most well-liked locations for glacier trekking, is situated in southern Iceland. It is renowned for having beautiful ice crevasses.

Ice climbing is what?

A more difficult sport, ice climbing requires mounting frozen waterfalls, glaciers, or ice cliffs with the use of specialized gear including crampons, ice axes, and ropes. Although it demands more technical skill and physical condition than glacier trekking, it offers a thrilling and memorable experience.

Where in Iceland can you go ice climbing?

Ice climbing is possible at several locations in Iceland, including:

Sólheimajökull Glacier: With its many climbable ice cliffs and frozen waterfalls, this glacier is also a well-liked location for ice climbing.

Mrdalsjökull Glacier: This glacier is home to several magnificent ice formations and provides some of Iceland's most difficult ice climbing.

The Vatnajökull Glacier is renowned for its breathtaking ice caves and has several ice climbing routes that are appropriate for both novice and expert climbers.

How can I hike glaciers and climb ice in Iceland?

In Iceland, there are various methods to undertake ice climbing and glacier hiking:

- Join a guided trip: Several tour companies in Iceland provide guided excursions for ice climbing and glacier trekking. These excursions provide knowledgeable tour leaders who can direct you to the finest locations and supply all essential gear.

- If you have prior glacier trekking or ice climbing expertise, you can hire equipment and independently explore Iceland's glaciers. Ice climbing and glacier trekking, however, should only be done by skilled people due to their potential for hazards.

Advice for ice climbing and glacier trekking in Iceland

- Dress appropriately: Ice climbing and glacier trekking both calls for warm, waterproof clothes as well as reliable hiking footwear. Additionally, don't forget to pack warm clothing such as hats, gloves, and scarves.

- If you're on a guided tour, pay close attention to your guide's instructions and pay attention to what they say. They are qualified experts that can assist keep you safe and make sure your trip is unforgettable.

- Be cautious of your surroundings and steer clear of any potentially unstable or dangerous regions since glaciers are always changing.

- Conserve the environment: Glaciers are delicate ecosystems that need caution and respect. Follow the designated pathways and don't damage the animals or the plants.

In general, Iceland's glacier trekking and ice climbing are fantastic activities that let you completely immerse yourself in the country's breathtaking natural splendor. To secure your safety and the safety of the environment, it is crucial to plan and take the required safeguards. Ice climbing and glacier trekking in Iceland may be a once-in-a-lifetime experience with the right preparation and direction.

Hot Springs and Thermal Pools

Visits to the many hot springs and thermal pools found in Iceland are among the most well-liked and distinctive outdoor pursuits. Iceland is home to a significant number of hot springs and thermal pools, ranging in size from tiny natural hot springs to big, built spa complexes, as a result of its volcanic activity and geothermal energy.

The Blue Lagoon, one of Iceland's most well-known hot springs, can be found on the Reykjanes Peninsula not far from Keflavik International Airport. A sizable, constructed spa complex called The Blue Lagoon allows guests to relax in warm, mineral-rich water while surrounded by breathtaking volcanic surroundings. The Blue Lagoon also provides a range of spa services, such as body wraps, facials, and massages.

The Secret Lagoon, another well-known hot spring in Iceland, is situated in the little town of Flir in the south of the country. A little spa complex has been built around a natural hot spring called The Secret Lagoon. Geothermal energy is used to warm the water in the Secret Lagoon, which is also full of minerals said to have therapeutic qualities.

There are several alternatives available if you want a hot spring experience that is more rural and natural. Reykjadalur, a natural hot spring that lies close to the town of Hverageri, is one of Iceland's most well-known hot springs. Popular hiking location Reykjadalur gives guests the option to relax in a naturally hot river while surrounded by breathtaking Icelandic scenery.

In Iceland's highlands, Landmannalaugar is yet another well-known natural hot spring. The only way to get to Landmannalaugar is with a four-wheel drive vehicle since it is a harsh and secluded place. The hot springs at Landmannalaugar provide guests with a one-of-a-kind and spectacular hot spring experience since they are surrounded by vibrant rhyolite mountains.

Iceland has a large number of thermal pools in addition to its hot springs, many of which are found in open-air swimming complexes around the nation. Laugardalslaug, a popular public swimming facility in Iceland, is situated in Reykjavik. A large, contemporary swimming facility called Laugardalslaug has a mix of indoor and outdoor pools in addition to hot tubs, saunas, and steam rooms.

Overall, taking a trip to Iceland requires you to see hot springs and thermal pools. Iceland has plenty to offer everyone, whether you're searching for an opulent spa experience or a more rustic, natural hot spring trip. To guarantee that future generations may enjoy these rare and priceless natural riches, just be sure to abide by local regulations and protect the environment.

Snowmobiling and Dog Sledding

Snowmobiling and dog sledding are just two of the thrilling outdoor pursuits available in Iceland's distinctive and untamed nature. These excursions enable tourists to take in the splendor of Iceland's winter wonderland while having exhilarating experiences that are certain to leave them with lifelong memories.

In Iceland, snowmobiling is a well-liked pastime that is accessible in several regions. Riding a snowmobile allows visitors to view glaciers and snow-covered areas. The second-largest glacier in Iceland, Langjökull, is one of the most well-liked places for snowmobiling. Snowmobilers may speed over the ice while providing visitors with panoramic views of the glacier. The biggest glacier in Iceland, Vatnajökull, as well as the South Iceland glacier Mrdalsjökull, which is renowned for its breathtaking ice tunnels, are other well-liked spots for snowmobiling.

Dog sledding is another well-liked outdoor pastime in Iceland. Visitors may enjoy a distinctive and traditional means of transportation while taking in the splendor of Iceland's winter scenery via dog sledding. Visitors may ride in a sled drawn by a team of skilled sled dogs and explore snow-covered mountains and woods. Visitors of all ages may enjoy the experience safely thanks to the sled dogs' friendliness and training.

There are several places in Iceland where you may go dog sledding, but some of the more well-liked spots are in South Iceland and on the Snaefellsnes Peninsula. Dog sledding experiences are available for visitors to select from, ranging from brief introduction tours to longer, multi-day adventures.

Both dog sledding and snowmobiling are well-liked pastimes in Iceland and are appropriate for tourists of all ability levels. However, to guarantee a secure and pleasurable experience, it's crucial to dress warmly and adhere to safety standards. To guarantee that Iceland's stunning and delicate landscapes are preserved for future generations, visitors should also practice environmental courtesy and the "Leave No Trace" philosophy.

To sum up, snowmobile and dog sledding are fun outdoor pursuits that let tourists take in Iceland's stunning winter scenery. These experiences are certain to leave guests of all ages with lifelong memories because of their knowledgeable guides and breathtaking settings. Snowmobiling and dog sledding in Iceland are not to be missed, whether you're a novice or an experienced explorer.

Skiing and Snowboarding

Although Iceland may not immediately spring to mind when you think of skiing and snowboarding, it nonetheless provides a distinctive and thrilling experience for fans of winter sports. Iceland is a fantastic location for skiing and snowboarding with a range of ski resorts and backcountry terrain.

Approximately a two-hour drive from Reykjavik, the Snaefellsnes Peninsula is home to Iceland's most well-known ski resort. The mountain resort has slopes for skiers and snowboarders of all abilities, as well as a terrain park for those who want to practice their jumps and rails skills.

In the north of Iceland, close to the city of Akureyri, lies another well-known ski area. For those seeking a more difficult experience, this resort provides backcountry terrain in addition to a range of slopes, some of the steepest in Iceland.

Iceland offers a wide variety of backcountry skiing and snowboarding opportunities. Some of Iceland's greatest backcountry skiing and snowboarding can be found in the isolated Westfjords area, which also has breathtaking views of the mountains and fjords nearby. Another well-liked location for backcountry skiing and snowboarding with a variety of slopes and terrain for all ability levels is the Eastern Rhyrningur mountain range.

It's vital to remember that skiing and snowboarding in Iceland may be difficult because of the erratic weather and shifting topography. To guarantee a secure and pleasurable trip, it is advised that guests hire an expert guide and come equipped with the right equipment and attire.

Iceland provides several additional winter sports, such as snowshoeing and cross-country skiing, in addition to skiing and snowboarding. Iceland's winter scenery may be explored on snowshoes because of the many routes that are accessible there. Many of Iceland's national parks include cross-country skiing paths, which is another well-liked winter sport.

In conclusion, Iceland offers thrilling outdoor pursuits like skiing and snowboarding. Skiers and snowboarders of all ability levels may find something to their liking thanks to the diversity of ski resorts and backcountry terrain. To guarantee a safe and pleasurable journey, it's crucial to be well-prepared and employ a knowledgeable guide.

Fishing and Sea Kayaking

In Iceland, fishing and sea kayaking are two well-liked outdoor pursuits that provide special chances to discover the nation's breathtakingly beautiful natural landscapes and marine life.

Both residents and visitors enjoy fishing in Iceland, where there are many different types of fishing to choose from. In many of Iceland's rivers and lakes, freshwater fishing is popular; regular catches include trout, salmon, and arctic char. Iceland's beaches provide possibilities to capture a variety of species, including cod, haddock, and halibut, for those seeking to try their hand at saltwater fishing. Numerous spots in Iceland offer fishing trips with knowledgeable operators who can provide equipment and advice to guarantee a good catch.

Another well-liked outdoor pastime in Iceland is sea kayaking, which provides a unique opportunity to see the nation's untamed fjords and rough coastline. In many areas in Iceland, kayaking trips are offered, ranging from leisurely paddles through beautiful scenery to more difficult adventures for more seasoned paddlers. A few trips also provide participants the chance to see marine caves and spot animals like seals and seagulls.

The Westfjords area, with its breathtaking fjords and uninhabited shoreline, is one of Iceland's most well-liked sea kayaking locations. The Snaefellsnes Peninsula, with its varied shoreline and breathtaking views of the Snfellsjökull glacier, is another well-liked vacation spot. Sea kayaking trips are offered to explore the rocky coastline and see natural marvels like glaciers and waterfalls along Iceland's south coast.

In Iceland, sea kayaking and fishing provide different adventures for outdoor lovers as well as chances to interact with the country's breathtaking natural beauty and marine life. Booking trips with knowledgeable tour leaders who can provide equipment and guarantee a fun and safe experience is crucial.

CHAPTER FIVE

Accommodations in Iceland

Hotels and Guesthouses

Since Iceland has recently gained popularity as a travel destination, a wide variety of lodging options are accessible to travelers. Iceland provides a variety of lodging alternatives, from five-star hotels to inexpensive guesthouses.

Icelandic lodging choices range from opulent five-star hotels to reasonably priced lodging. The majority of hotels in Iceland are found in or close to the country's largest towns, including Reykjavik, Akureyri, and Keflavik, however, some are also found in farther-flung locales like the highlands or the Westfjords. Some of Iceland's most opulent hotels include services like spas, fine dining restaurants, and picturesque views of the surroundings. Other hotels could have fewer amenities, but they still provide visitors with decent lodging.

Iceland provides a range of guesthouses in addition to hotels for those searching for more affordable accommodation. In Iceland, guesthouses are often smaller, family-run businesses that provide standard facilities like private bedrooms and common bathrooms. Numerous guesthouses are found in rural locations, allowing tourists to enjoy Iceland's breathtaking natural beauty in a more private environment.

The act of camping is another well-liked lodging choice in Iceland. Many camping areas can be found all around Iceland, making it an inexpensive choice for those who wish to be more in tune with nature. Many campgrounds include basic services like bathrooms and showers, and some may even have kitchens that visitors may use.

Iceland also has a range of specialty lodging options, including farm stays, glacier huts, and even igloos, for those looking for a more singular experience. These kinds of lodgings provide guests an opportunity to immerse themselves more fully in Iceland's distinctive scenery and culture.

No matter the kind of lodging you choose in Iceland, it's crucial to reserve early, particularly during the busiest tourist times. To make sure your selected lodgings fit your wants and expectations, it's also crucial to explore their location and features. Iceland offers a wide range of lodging options, so visitors may choose the one that best suits their needs both financially and in terms of travel style.

Hostels and Budget Options

Hostels and other inexpensive lodging alternatives may be an excellent way for tourists on a tight budget to save costs while still taking advantage of everything that Iceland has to offer.

Icelandic hostels include both private rooms with en-suite bathrooms and dormitory-style rooms with common restrooms. Numerous hostels also include community places for visitors to unwind and mingle, such as common halls and shared kitchens. Some hostels even have their bars and restaurants, providing guests with a variety of inexpensive food alternatives.

Meeting other visitors from all over the globe is one of the advantages of staying in a hostel. Backpackers, lone travelers, families, and groups of friends are just a few of the many types of tourists that hostels often draw. The chance to share travel advice and meet new people may create a lively and sociable environment.

In addition to hostels, Iceland offers guesthouses, campgrounds, and even couch surfing as alternative low-cost lodging choices. In Iceland, guesthouses are mainly modest, family-run businesses that provide private rooms with common toilets. For tourists who want a bit more solitude than a hostel but still want to keep expenses low, this might be a wonderful alternative.

In Iceland, camping is another well-liked low-cost holiday choice. The nation provides a wide variety of permitted camping locations, from simple ones with simply a toilet and a water supply to more sophisticated ones with showers and kitchens. Camping may be an excellent way to take in Iceland's natural beauty up close and for a lot less money than other forms of lodging.

Another low-cost vacation option in Iceland is Couchsurfing. This entails spending free time at the house of a local host in return for socializing and participating in cultural activities. While choosing this option might be a terrific way to meet people and save money, it's crucial to ensure that your host is respectable and reliable.

Overall, Iceland provides tourists with a selection of reasonably priced lodging options. Hostels and other inexpensive lodging choices may be an excellent way to save costs while still enjoying all Iceland has to offer. To avoid disappointment, make your reservations as soon as possible, particularly during busy travel times. To be sure that your selected lodgings fit your requirements and expectations, be sure to explore their location and features.

Camping in Iceland

In Iceland, camping is a well-liked and reasonably priced method to take in the natural beauty of the place. The nation offers several places that are specifically allocated for camping, from simple locations with simply a restroom and a water supply to more developed locations with showers, kitchens, and even swimming pools.

The chance to fully experience Iceland's breathtaking scenery is one of the advantages of camping there. Numerous camping sites are found in or close to national parks, glaciers, waterfalls, and other scenic landmarks. This enables visitors to spend less on lodging while yet being near these natural treasures.

Travelers who like outdoor pursuits like hiking, fishing, and birding might consider camping. As a result of the remoteness of many of the camping locations, visitors may explore Iceland's wilderness on foot or by bicycle. There are even more options for adventure at certain campgrounds, which also include activities like horseback riding and rafting.

Camping in Iceland may be economical and enjoyable, as well as sociable. Many of the campgrounds provide community spaces with kitchens, BBQs, and picnic tables that let visitors interact and make new friends. Even some campgrounds have their cafés and restaurants, providing a handy choice for dining.

Being weather-ready is essential while camping in Iceland. Even in the summertime, temperatures in the nation may be chilly, and rain is often seen. To have a relaxing camping trip, remember to pack warm clothes, rain gear, and a strong tent.

It's also crucial to remember that Iceland forbids wild camping. Travelers are required to camp only in approved locations, clean up after themselves, and leave the area in the same state as when they arrived. Additionally, it's crucial to abide by any guidelines established by the particular camping location, such as prohibitions on fires and quiet hours.

Overall, camping in Iceland may be a satisfying and cost-effective way to take in the natural beauty of the place. However, it's crucial to dress for the weather and abide by the guidelines set out by the permitted camping locations. Camping in Iceland may be a memorable and delightful experience if you plan and prepare well.

CHAPTER SIX

Dining and Nightlife in Iceland

Traditional Icelandic Cuisine

Traditional Icelandic food emphasizes the use of fresh, locally obtained ingredients and is a distinctive fusion of Nordic and European tastes. Due to Iceland's remoteness and severe environment, its culinary traditions have evolved to emphasize food preservation and the use of every animal's parts.

Here are some examples of the traditional foods and ingredients you may find in Iceland.

Fish: It should come as no surprise that fish is a mainstay of Icelandic cuisine given the country's 4,970 km of coastline. Haddock that has been grilled or fried, salmon soup, and pickled herring are some of the most well-liked fish meals. Arctic char and cod are just two of the unusual and delectable fish species that call Iceland's frigid, clean waters home.

Lamb: Sheep farming is a significant business in Iceland, and dishes like lamb soup and smoked lamb often use lamb as an ingredient. The animal's diet of wild grasses and herbs is the reason the meat is prized for its softness and distinctive taste.

Skyr: Skyr is a traditional dairy product from Iceland that resembles yogurt but has a creamier, thicker texture. It is often eaten as a breakfast dish with fresh fruit and oats or as a dessert with a sweetener like honey or sugar.

Rye bread: A mainstay of Icelandic cooking, rye bread is often made using geothermal energy in old-fashioned earth ovens known as "hverabrau." The substantial, somewhat sweet, thick bread is often served with butter and smoked salmon.

Shark that has been fermented: Not for the timid! The flesh of the Greenland shark is used to make the traditional Icelandic delicacy known as "hákarl," or fermented shark. For many months, the shark flesh is buried in the ground to ferment, after which it is hung to dry. It tastes strongly like ammonia and has an awful odor.

Iceland boasts a dynamic culinary culture that combines worldwide tastes and techniques in addition to these traditional cuisines. Particularly in

Reykjavik, there is a thriving nightlife with a selection of eateries, pubs, and cafés. **Several well-liked** Restaurants **are:**

Matur og Drykkur: This eatery serves up modern interpretations of classic Icelandic fare, like lamb shoulder and cured fish.

Grillmarkaurinn is a restaurant with a focus on grilled meats and seafood that employs foods that are produced locally. It is situated in the heart of Reykjavik.

The Sea Baron: This seafood stand on the port in Reykjavik is well-known for its grilled fish skewers and lobster soup.

Cafe Babal is a popular place for breakfast or lunch and offers handmade pastries, sandwiches, and coffee.

Micro Bar: This establishment has a large range of craft beers from across the world and Iceland, as well as a welcoming environment and helpful personnel.

Everyone can find something to enjoy in Iceland's eating and nightlife scene, whether they want to sample traditional Icelandic food or discover the nation's contemporary culinary culture.

Vegetarian and Vegan Options

In recent years, Iceland has made great strides in its efforts to accommodate vegetarians and vegans. The nation, which was once recognized for its dependence on meat and fish, is now a popular destination for individuals looking for plant-based cuisine alternatives. Vegetarians and vegans may choose from a wide range of enticing and nourishing cuisine alternatives, from hip eateries in Reykjavik to neighborhood cafés in the countryside.

The focus on local, fresh foods in Iceland's vegetarian and vegan culture is one of its greatest features. Because of its geographical position, Iceland has a peculiar growing season, which means that a lot of the product is produced in geothermal greenhouses, giving it a distinct flavor. Numerous vegetarian and vegan cuisines in Iceland feature these year-round, geothermally-grown plants including tomatoes, cucumbers, and bell peppers.

The capital of Iceland, Reykjavik, is home to a large selection of vegetarian and vegan eateries, cafés, and pubs. Kaffi Vnyl, one of the most well-known vegan eateries in Reykjavik, offers plant-based variations of traditional Icelandic cuisine such as meatballs and fish & chips. Another well-liked alternative is Gló, which provides a selection of hot entrees, soups, and salads produced with organic and regionally grown products.

Icelandic petrol stations are a surprisingly nice alternative for vegetarians and vegans searching for a fast snack. It is simple to obtain food on the fly since so many gas stations sell prepared salads and sandwiches that are marked as vegan or vegetarian.

Vegetarian and vegan choices are still widely available outside of Reykjavik. For instance, there is a quaint little vegetarian restaurant called Graenn Kostur in the little town of Akureyri that offers delectable plant-based cuisine. Additionally, farm-to-table eateries like Friheimar, which specializes in tomato-based meals, provide a distinctive and delectable eating experience in the countryside.

Reykjavik boasts a thriving bar culture that offers lots of alternatives for vegetarians and vegans. Numerous bars and pubs provide vegetarian and vegan bar fare like falafel or hummus platters, and some even have vegan full-course menus. For instance, Kex Hostel provides a well-liked vegan cuisine with items like a vegan burger and vegan tacos.

Vegans and vegetarians may feel secure knowing that Iceland provides a wide variety of alternatives for them. Iceland has developed into a fantastic location for anybody looking for excellent and healthful vegetarian and vegan cuisine alternatives thanks to a focus on fresh, local foods and a rising number of plant-based restaurants and cafés.

Best Bars and Nightclubs

Iceland's vibrant bars and nightclubs live music venues, and late-night cafes make it one of the most interesting nightlife scenes in Europe. Iceland has plenty to offer everyone, whether you're searching for a warm pub to relax in after a long day of touring or a dance floor to party the night away.

Iceland's capital city, Reykjavik, is the center of the nation's nightlife culture. With little over 120,000 residents, the city features an unexpectedly high number of pubs and clubs, ranging from laid-back and posh to fashionable and expensive. The following are a few of Reykjavik's top bars:

Kaffibarinn is a well-known bar with a hip and fashionable atmosphere that is situated in the center of downtown Reykjavik. The pub often holds live music events and offers a wide variety of regional beers and beverages.

Priki: One of Reykjavik's oldest pubs, Priki was founded in 1951 and is known for being the place to go for a night out. The pub has a reputation for having a fun environment, great drinks, and late-night food.

Beer connoisseurs love **Mikkeller & Friends,** a craft beer establishment that serves a variety of domestic and imported beers. With a fireplace and nice seats, the bar also boasts a warm environment.

In addition to pubs, Reykjavik is home to several nightclubs that are well-liked by both residents and visitors. **The following are a few of the Top Clubs in Reykjavik:**

Austur is a posh nightclub in the center of Reykjavik that is well-known for its chic décor, pricey cocktails, and celebrity sightings.

The stylish **Vesturbaer** district is home to the hip club Hrra, which is well-known for its diverse clientele and live music events.

Paloma - This club, which is housed in a former movie theater, is renowned for its retro-chic furnishings, themed events, and all-night dancing.

There are several pubs and nightclubs in various towns and cities around Iceland besides Reykjavik. For instance, there are various pubs and clubs in the town of Akureyri in the north of Iceland, including Akureyri Backpackers and Hafnarstrti 9. Gamli Baukur and Salka are only a few of the taverns and pubs in the northern town of Hsavk.

Overall, anybody wishing to let loose and have a good time can find a wide variety of alternatives in Iceland's nightlife scene. There is something for everyone in this bustling and interesting nation, from quaint taverns to upscale nightclubs.

CHAPTER SEVEN

Practical Information for Travelers

Language and Communication

The majority of people in Iceland speak Icelandic, which is the country's official tongue. But English is extensively used and understood throughout the nation, especially in the travel and tourism sector. Other languages spoken by many Icelanders include Danish, German, French, and Spanish.

Although speaking Icelandic is not a requirement for tourists, it is usually appreciated when foreigners make an effort to acquire a few fundamental words and phrases. Travelers may find the following phrases in Icelandic useful:

Góðan daginn (Good day)
Bless (Goodbye)
Já (Yes)
Nei (No)
Takk (Thank you)
Verðið þið sael (Goodbye to more than one person)

It's crucial to be respectful and kind while speaking with natives. Although they are renowned for being amiable and helpful, Icelanders may sometimes be reticent and secretive. Instead of using someone's last name or title, it is usual to address them by their first name.

Iceland's telecommunications network is up-to-date and dependable in terms of communication infrastructure. Excellent mobile phone service is available across the nation, and tourists may simply obtain prepaid SIM cards from companies like Vodafone, Siminn, and Nova.

The majority of hotels, cafés, and restaurants in Iceland provide free Wi-Fi to clients, and the country also boasts a sophisticated internet infrastructure. Additionally, there are several areas around the nation with public Wi-Fi hotspots, including airports, bus terminals, and tourist information offices.

Iceland has a thorough system in place for emergency services to guarantee the security of both its residents and tourists. 112, which may be called from any phone, even mobile devices without a SIM card, is the nation's emergency number. The service is free, and the staff members are bilingual and fluent in English.

Since English is widely spoken and understood in Iceland, communication is normally not a big problem for visitors. However, being familiar with certain fundamental Icelandic idioms and practices may help tourists interact with people and demonstrate their interest in Icelandic culture.

Safety and Security

In general, travelers find Iceland to be a safe and secure destination. There is very little violent crime in the nation. There are still certain safety issues, nevertheless, that travelers should be aware of, just as in any other trip location.

The weather in Iceland is one of the main safety concerns for visitors. Iceland's weather is erratic and sometimes severe, especially in the winter. If visitors want to participate in outdoor activities like hiking or skiing, they should dress for chilly weather, brisk winds, and plenty of snow. It's crucial to dress correctly and have the right accessories, such as durable shoes and waterproof apparel.

Iceland's rough landscape is another issue for travelers' safety there. Iceland's natural beauty is a big magnet for tourists, but it can also be risky. Visitors should always be mindful of their surroundings while trekking, particularly in isolated locations, and they should never undervalue the might of Iceland's glaciers and waterfalls. Always adhere to designated paths and local authorities and tour guides' instructions while visiting.

In addition to natural threats, travelers should be on the lookout for scams and other types of small-time crime. Even though Iceland has a low crime rate, pickpockets and other criminals may sometimes target travelers, particularly in busy tourist locations. When using ATMs and transferring money, visitors should keep their belongings safe and exercise caution.

Iceland is typically a safe place to go about health and medical issues. Visitors may get medical care in hospitals and clinics all around the nation because of the excellent level of healthcare there. Visitors should still use common sense health measures like washing their hands often, drinking plenty of water, and getting enough sleep to keep healthy.

Additionally, tourists need to have proper travel insurance since uninsured patients may incur high costs for medical care in Iceland. In the case of a major sickness or accident, visitors should confirm that emergency medical evacuation is covered by their insurance.

Overall, Iceland is a welcome and safe tourist destination. Visitors should nevertheless be cautious and take simple safety measures, particularly while indulging in outdoor activities or traveling to distant locations. Visitors may fully take advantage of all Iceland has to offer by being aware of possible hazards and taking precautions to be safe.

Health and Medical Services

Visitors may get medical care at hospitals and clinics located all around Iceland, which offer good quality healthcare. All visitors are entitled to free emergency medical care, and the nation's healthcare system is publicly sponsored.

Iceland is home to several hospitals and medical facilities, including one in Reykjavik, the capital of the nation. Many of these clinics feature up-to-date medical facilities and equipment, and they are manned by qualified medical experts. The nation is home to several private medical offices, pharmacies, and hospitals in addition to clinics and hospitals.

Because medical care in Iceland may be costly for those without insurance, travelers should make sure they have proper travel insurance. In the case of a major sickness or accident, visitors should confirm that emergency medical evacuation is covered by their insurance.

Visitors may get care for minor ailments or wounds at a neighborhood pharmacy, called "apótek" in Icelandic. These pharmacies often have professional pharmacists working inside who may provide advice and prescribe medicine for common conditions including colds, allergies, and minor accidents.

Additionally, there are some health concerns in Iceland that travelers should be aware of, including exposure to the cold, exposure to volcanic gases and ash, and foodborne infections. Basic health measures like regular hand washing, drinking enough water, and getting adequate sleep should be taken by visitors.

Visitors may dial 112, Iceland's emergency services number, in case of a medical emergency. If required, the operator will be able to send out emergency medical assistance.

Iceland's healthcare system is generally of good quality, and travelers may get medical attention anywhere in the nation. Visitors should make sure they have proper travel insurance and take simple health measures, but they may rest easy knowing that medical care is easily accessible if necessary.

Tipping and Etiquette

Understanding Icelandic conventions and etiquette, particularly tipping regulations, is crucial when organizing a vacation there. Here is a handbook to help you understand Icelandic tipping customs and manners.

Tipping: In Iceland, leaving a gratuity is neither customary nor expected. Though it is not customary, you might leave a little tip if you feel that the service was extraordinary or if you just want to express your gratitude. Tipping is not required since a service fee is often added to the bill at restaurants, cafés, and pubs.

It is customary, but again, not expected, to round up the fee in a cab to the next whole number. Hairdressers often get tips, although other service sectors do not need them.

Etiquette: Icelanders are often courteous, restrained, and kind when it comes to etiquette. Here are some general pointers to remember:

Icelanders shake hands and make eye contact when they meet one another. Additionally, greetings are often exchanged before a conversation's primary purpose.

Icelanders are frequently on time and appreciate punctuality. Be careful to appear on time if you've been invited to a meeting or function.

Icelanders appreciate their privacy and may maintain a distance while conversing with others. They also tend to be quiet and avoid chit-chatting with strangers.

When it comes to apparel, Icelanders place high importance on comfort and practicality. Because the weather may be erratic and the terrain might be rough, it's best to dress in layers and wear comfortable shoes.

Icelanders like to drink, but they usually do so in moderation. It's also customary to raise a glass and exclaim *"skál"*. (cheers) when everyone has been served.

Icelanders have great regard for the environment and the natural world. To help protect these stunning locations for future generations, be careful to abide by the laws and regulations while visiting natural sites.

Icelanders are generally kind, inviting, and accommodating to guests. You may make sure that your vacation to Iceland is enjoyable and memorable by paying attention to these suggestions and observing regional traditions.

CHAPTER EIGHT

Useful Phrases in Icelandic

Greetings and Introductions

Although English is widely spoken by Icelanders, Icelandic is the country's official language, thus it is always appreciated when tourists make an effort to acquire a few fundamental words. Every society values introductions and greetings, and Iceland is no exception. The following words and phrases can come in handy while meeting people in Iceland:

Hello - Halló
The most typical greeting in Icelandic, it may be used in both official and casual contexts.

Good morning - Góðan daginn
Up to noon, this salutation is utilized.

Good afternoon - Góðan dag
Between lunchtime and early evening, this salutation is employed.

Good evening - Gott kvöld
In the late evening and into the night, this greeting is employed.

Goodbye - Bless
The most typical form of farewell in Icelandic is this.

See you later - Sjáumst seinna
This expression is often used when bidding on a person farewell who you want to see again.

Nice to meet you - Gaman að kynnast þér
This is a formal way to say that you are happy to meet someone for the first time.

My name is... - Ég heiti...
To introduce yourself, say this.

What is your name? - Hvað heitir þú?
When meeting someone for the first time, this is a typical question to ask.

Where are you from? - Hvaðan ertu?
People often ask this question in informal conversations.

It is crucial to remember that regardless of age or rank, Icelanders often refer to one another by their first names. However, it is polite to address them by their last name while speaking to them informally or when you don't know them well.

Although close friends and relatives may embrace or kiss on the cheek, shaking hands is also a frequent welcome in Iceland. Maintaining eye contact and demonstrating respect for the person you are conversing with is crucial.

Your journey to Iceland will likely be more pleasurable if you learn a few simple Icelandic words. You may interact with locals and get a greater understanding of this distinctive and stunning nation by demonstrating an interest in the language and culture.

Ordering Food and Drinks

Icelandic, which is the country's official language, is a North Germanic tongue that has some kinship with other Scandinavian languages like Norwegian, Danish, and Swedish. However, English is a common language in Iceland and is spoken there often. However, knowing a few Icelandic words may tremendously improve your trip to Iceland, especially when it comes to ordering food and beverages. Here are some helpful Icelandic expressions for placing food and beverage orders in Iceland:

✚ "Má ég fá," which means "May I have,"
When placing an order in a restaurant or café, this statement might be helpful. "Má ég fá kaffi og

kleinu?" is one example. (May I please have a pastry and coffee?)

+ "Eitt af þessu, takk." - "Please, one of these."

When you wish to order something that is already on display, this statement comes in helpful. For instance, while pointing to a pastry, you would say, "Eitt af essu, takk" (One of these, please).

+ "Hvað maelið þið með?" - What would you suggest?

If you are unclear about what to purchase and would want some guidance, this expression might be helpful. "Hva mli i me af fiskréttum," for instance. (What meal do you suggest for fish?)

+ "Er þetta með..." - Are these served with?

When you want to know what comes with your dinner, this expression is useful. "Er etta me braui?" is an example. (Is bread included with this?)

+ "Gætirðu kveikt á ljósin?" Can you please turn on the lights?

When trying to read the menu at a dark café or restaurant, this expression may be helpful. As in the phrase "Gtiru kveikt á ljósin?" Please turn on the lights.

- "Má ég fá rjóma?" - "Can I please have some cream?"

If you want to add cream to your coffee or dessert, use this phrase. "Má ég fá rjóma kaffi mitt," for instance. Please add some cream to my coffee.

- "Hvað er í þessu drykki?" - "What's in this drink, exactly?"

When you want to know the contents of a certain drink, this statement might be useful. "Hva er essu kokteili," for instance. What's in this drink, exactly?

- "Gott að smakk!" - "Enjoy your meal!"

It's polite to say "Have a good meal" to someone. Say, "Gott a smakk!" for instance. (Spend time eating!)

Overall, being able to order food and beverages in Iceland may be greatly aided by understanding a few simple Icelandic words. The Icelandic people are renowned for their friendliness and kindness, and they often offer to assist guests with their linguistic needs. Therefore, don't be shy about using your Icelandic while savoring some of Iceland's delectable foods and beverages.

Asking for Directions

Here are some typical ways to request directions:

⊥ "Hvar er...?"
The simplest method to ask for directions is to say,
"Where is..." After the phrase, you may add the name
of the location you're searching for.

⊥ "Ég er tndur/ tnd" (I am lost) is a phrase you
may use to ask for directions if you find
yourself in a perplexing region.

⊥ It's helpful to know the phrase "Fara beint
áfram" (Go straight ahead) when someone is
giving you instructions. This expression
implies "go straight ahead" since "beint
áfram" denotes a direction.

⊥ The expression "Beygja til haegri/vinstri"
(Turn right/left) is also crucial for giving and
receiving instructions.

⊥ "Hversu langt er það?" (How far is it?): This
query may be used to determine a location's
distance.

⊥ "Á hvaða hótel/veitingarstað er það nálægt?"
What hotel or lodging establishment is

vacant? (What restaurant or motel is nearby?) You may use this inquiry to get advice on what's around if you're curious about a certain place.

- ↓ "Geturðu tekið kortið/vegaseðilinn með þér?" (Can you bring the instructions and/or a map with you?) You may use this expression to request permission to take the map or instructions with you while someone is giving you directions.

It's essential to keep in mind that Icelandic has complicated grammar and distinctive sounds. If you find it tough to master, don't give up. Knowing a few words and phrases in Icelandic is only a way to show respect for the native way of life as most Icelanders are delighted to speak English with visitors.

Emergency Phrases

Although Iceland is a secure nation, it's always a good idea to be ready for emergencies, particularly if you want to visit any of its more isolated regions. You can interact with locals and get the assistance you want in an emergency by learning a few simple Icelandic words and phrases. The following emergency words and phrases exist in Icelandic:

⊕ Hjálp! (Help!) - This is the most basic emergency phrase and can be used to call for help in any situation.

⊕ Ég þarf hjálp (I need help) - This phrase can be used to explain what kind of help you need, such as if you are injured, lost, or in danger.

⊕ Ég er í neyð (I am in distress) - This phrase can be used to indicate that you are in a serious emergency and need immediate assistance.

⊕ Símið í lögregluna er 112 (The emergency number for the police is 112) - 112 is the emergency number in Iceland that can be used to call for police, fire, or ambulance services.

⊕ Ég er sár (I am injured) - This phrase can be used to explain that you have sustained an injury and need medical attention.

- Ég er frosinn (I am cold) - This phrase can be used to explain that you are experiencing hypothermia and need to warm up.

- Ég er laestur úti (I am locked out) - This phrase can be used if you have been locked out of your car or accommodation and need assistance.

- Ég er tapaður (I am lost) - This phrase can be used to explain that you are lost and need help finding your way.

- Ég hef misst mitt farartæki (I have lost my vehicle) - This phrase can be used if you have lost your rental car or another mode of transportation.

- Ég hef misst minn reisnarskuld (I have lost my passport) - This phrase can be used if you have lost your passport or other important documents.

Keep in mind that Icelanders are often quite kind and helpful, and they will do their best to aid you if you need it. To guarantee that you can communicate successfully in an emergency, it is always better to be organized and have a basic grasp of the local tongue.

CHAPTER NINE

Conclusion and Additional Resources

Final Thoughts on Iceland

Iceland is a distinctive and intriguing holiday destination with a wealth of outdoor recreation opportunities. There are many opportunities for adventure and breathtaking experiences, such as visiting glaciers, lagoons, hot springs, and the Northern Lights.

To guarantee a safe and pleasurable vacation, it's crucial to do the necessary research and preparation before making travel plans to Iceland. This entails being aware of any safety problems and emergency protocols, as well as learning about regional traditions and etiquette.

Having a working knowledge of Icelandic is also advantageous since many locals may not be proficient in English. Understanding the customary greetings, ways to order food and beverages, and ways to ask for directions will make traveling the nation much simpler.

Travelers wanting to plan their trip to Iceland have access to a wide range of online and physical resources in addition to those included in this guide. Tourism organizations, travel websites, and travel guides may all give insightful advice on how to enjoy Iceland to the fullest.

Iceland is a unique and spectacular tourist destination that has something to offer every kind of visitor, in general. Iceland is a country that will make a lasting effect on anybody who comes, from the breathtaking scenery to the friendly people and rich culture.

Recommended Reading and Websites

Iceland is a distinctive and alluring location with a wide range of things to do and sights to see. There are several tools at your disposal to assist you in making the most of your time in Iceland, whether you're planning a quick vacation or a longer stay.

The official Icelandic tourist website, http://www.visiticeland.com, is a fantastic resource. You may learn more about lodgings, activities, events, and more right here. You may subscribe to their newsletter to get updates on the newest information and offers, as well as request brochures and maps.

Finally, we strongly suggest the website http://www.safetravel.is for people who want to drive in Iceland. This website offers current details on the state of the roads, the weather, and other dangers, as well as recommendations for safe driving in Iceland.

Finally, Iceland is a genuinely amazing place that has something to offer every tourist. Iceland is certain to make an impact, whether you want to discover its natural treasures, immerse yourself in its distinct culture, or just take in its breathtaking scenery and exciting nightlife. You can maximize your time in Iceland and build lifelong experiences with a little planning and preparation.

Contact Information and Resources

A journey to Iceland should be well-planned and researched before leaving. Here are some helpful links and phone numbers to help you plan a successful trip:

Icelandic Tourist Board: This government-run company provides thorough information on visiting Iceland, including information on attractions, lodgings, and transit choices.

The http://www.visiticeland.com website is a great place to start when organizing your vacation.

Icelandic Road Administration: This organization is in charge of keeping the nation's roads in good condition and providing information about road closures. Anyone who intends to drive in Iceland may find helpful information on their website, http://www.road.is.

Icelandic Meteorological Office: This organization offers current information on Iceland's meteorological conditions, including alerts and warnings for dangerous weather conditions. Travelers who wish to remain up to date on the weather might consult their website, http://www.vedur.is.

This volunteer-run group, Icelandic Search and Rescue, offers search and rescue services throughout Iceland. Call the emergency services at 112, and they will, if required, collaborate with Icelandic Search and Rescue, in the case of an emergency.

Icelandic Red Cross: This group offers ambulance and medical services along with first aid and emergency assistance. Information about first aid training programs and other training possibilities

may   be   found   on   their
website, http://www.redcross.is.

Iceland is a fascinating and distinctive holiday
destination with a variety of natural wonders and
cultural attractions to discover. Visitors may make
the most of their stay in this lovely nation with the
right forethought and preparation.

Printed in Great Britain
by Amazon